Gustav Klimt
Egon Schiele

Plate 1. Egon Schiele. *Autumn Sun (Sunrise)*. 1912.

Gustav Klimt
Egon Schiele

Jane Kallir

Foreword by Thomas M. Messer
With a Tribute by Alessandra Comini

In Commemoration of the Achievements of Dr. Otto Kallir

A Herbert Michelman Book
Galerie St. Etienne/Crown Publishers, Inc.
New York

Exhibition dates:
November 11–December 27, 1980
Galerie St. Etienne
24 West 57th Street
New York, New York 10019

Inquiries should be addressed to Crown Publishers, Inc., One Park Avenue, New York, New York 10016

Published simultaneously in Canada by General Publishing Company Limited

Library of Congress Cataloging in Publication Data
Main entry under title:
Gustav Klimt—Egon Schiele: in commemoration of the achievements of Dr. Otto Kallir.

Exhibition held at the Galerie St. Etienne, New York City, Nov. 11–Dec. 27, 1980.

"A Herbert Michelman book."

1. Klimt, Gustav, 1862–1918—Exhibitions. 2. Schiele, Egon, 1890–1918—Exhibitions. 3. Kallir, Otto, 1894–1978. I. Klimt, Gustav, 1862–1918. II. Schiele, Egon, 1890–1918. III. Kallir, Jane. IV. Galerie St. Etienne, New York.
ND511.5.K55A4   1980   759.36′074′01471   80-22018
ISBN: 0-517-54234X

10 9 8 7 6 5 4 3 2 1

Designed by Gary Cosimini
Printed by Rapoport Printing Corp., New York

Front cover: Egon Schiele. *Woman in Green Blouse with Muff.* 1915.
Back cover: Gustav Klimt. *Pear Tree.* 1903, later worked over.

Acknowledgments

WE WOULD LIKE to express our heartfelt thanks to the many people who have made this project possible, first and foremost to the museums and collectors who so generously lent works to the exhibition. Special thanks go to Dr. Vita M. Künstler and Mrs. Fanny Kallir for their enormous help in retracing the historical and biographical background for the book, and to Thomas M. Messer, Director of the Solomon R. Guggenheim Museum, and Alessandra Comini, Professor of Art History at Southern Methodist University, for their contributions. Also, a word of appreciation to Dr. Hans Aurenhammer, Director of the Oesterreichische Galerie, and Dr. Alice Strobl of the Albertina Museum for their continuing interest and support. Finally, mention must be made of Herbert Michelman of Crown Publishers, who went out of his way to make this book a reality.

Hildegard Bachert
Jane Kallir
Directors, Galerie St. Etienne

Honorary Committee

for the Otto Kallir Memorial Exhibition Series

Contents

Foreword
by Thomas M. Messer 9

Hands across the Water: A Tribute to Dr. Otto Kallir
by Alessandra Comini 11

Kallir, Klimt and Schiele
by Jane Kallir 15

Gustav Klimt:
A Chronology 28

Egon Schiele:
A Chronology 30

The Plates 32

List of Plates 90

Notes 94

List of Exhibitions 95

Foreword

by Thomas M. Messer

I REMEMBER one morning when I was awakened by a rather early telephone call at the Harvard Club in New York, where I used to stay when visiting from Boston. It was February, 1961, and I had just been appointed Director of the Guggenheim Museum. The call was from Dr. Otto Kallir, who, having just read the early city edition of the *New York Times*, was the first among those not privy to the appointment to congratulate me while I was still crossing the threshold dividing deep sleep from wakeful awareness. But I perked up as Dr. Kallir moved quickly from polite expressions to more substantial matters. "You are Director of the Guggenheim Museum and you like Schiele," began his irrefutable premise . . . and there was indeed little more to be added. Four years later—none too long for a major undertaking—a big Schiele show was winding up the ramps of my Museum, yielding, for good measure, into a small but impressive selection of rare paintings by Gustav Klimt.

It was neither my first nor my last collaboration with this redoubtable scholar/dealer, whose activities at the Galerie St. Etienne had intrigued me ever since I returned from the war in the late 1940s. As a result of this exposure (and then greatly dependent upon Dr. Kallir), I opened in 1960 Schiele's first American museum show at the Institute of Contemporary Art in Boston, which I directed at that time. A decade and a half thereafter (now much more independently, but still in valued collaboration with the Director of the St. Etienne gallery and his faithful aide Hildegard Bachert), I staged a Schiele retrospective at Munich's *Haus der Kunst. "Aller guten Dinge sind drei,"*—all good things come threefold, as Dr. Kallir maintained.

None of these undertakings came easily, partly because Dr. Kallir was not an easy person to deal with. His scholarship in the field of his specialization was deeply rooted and fully supported by participatory presence in an era that had since become historic. His standards, particularly with regard to factuality, were correspondingly exacting, and his impatience with anything less than perfect was not even superficially concealed. Keenly competitive, fussy about detail, and unaccommodating in the face of adversely developing situations, he would sit it out until things were just right. But the results eventually would bear him out, and what he sold, published, or showed, whether one agreed or disagreed with individual choices, always bore the mark of an authentic, deeply felt, even willful conviction which, at its best, led to high attainment and extraordinary distinction.

Just to return to personal contacts once more: I knew Schiele's major portrait, the so-called *Old Man* (the artist's father-in-law, Johann Harms) (Pl. 48), when it hung in the St. Etienne gallery at a time when prices for Schiele paintings were a fraction of today's values. Two decades and thousands of dollars later, the painting finally ended up in the Guggenheim's permanent collection, the financial load somewhat lessened by Dr. Kallir's partial donation thereof, perhaps to reimburse me for some of the pain that the gradual escalation caused me while I was reaching for the desired item like Tantalus for the ever-beckoning and ever-elusive fruit. But never mind. Schiele's masterpiece at the Guggenheim joins Kokoschka's *Knight Errant*, which belonged to Dr. Kallir at one time. To my regret, the third of the *drei guten Dinge* got away after an equally prolonged effort. Gustav Klimt's *Baby* (Pl. 52), now at the National Gallery in Washington, D.C., had also been a part of Dr. Kallir's collection.

Hands across the Water:
A Tribute to Dr. Otto Kallir

by Alessandra Comini

Dr. OTTO KALLIR, citizen of Austria for the first forty-four years of his life, and of the United States for the last thirty-nine years, was surely a remarkable, though unofficial, Ambassador-at-Large for Austrian Art. When he died at the age of eighty-four on November 30, 1978, his vital role in the worldwide recognition now afforded the painters Gustav Klimt, Richard Gerstl, and Egon Schiele had indeed been acknowledged by the land of his birth: the Republic of Austria and the City of Vienna had both awarded medals of honor to this distinguished former subject of Kaiser Franz Josef's Austro-Hungarian Empire. Born in Vienna on April 1, 1894—just eight years after Kokoschka and four years after Schiele—Dr. Kallir, like the Viennese artists and authors he championed, contended all his life with the love-hate response for which Vienna—birthplace of psychoanalysis—is famous. From his achievements as a publisher (*Johannes Presse*) of contemporary authors (Hofmannsthal, Rilke, Thomas Mann, Max Mell) through four decades devoted to documenting the art of Schiele (first oeuvre catalogue of paintings, 1930; second, enlarged and revised edition, 1966; oeuvre catalogue of the graphic work, 1970), labyrinthine byways awaited his efforts. Time and again his investigations encountered that ubiquitous Austrian attitude summed up by the adage *"Warum einfach, wenn es kompliziert geht?"* (Why do it simply when it can be made complicated?) In spite of the complications and even occasional deliberate hindrances in his path, Dr. Kallir succeeded, through many skillful transatlantic maneuvers, in preserving not only the works but also the reputations of Austrian artists who, as their fame abroad grew, suffered the attendant problems of misattribution and forgery. All his life Dr. Kallir sought to abolish the *Tratsch* (gossip), as he called it, in art and render justice to the integrity of the art work.

THE QUALITY of that art work—as represented by the images reproduced in this book—was not only compelling but of vital cultural importance. In focusing his aesthetic attention upon the works of Klimt and Schiele, Dr. Kallir documented two contiguous but radically different epochs of Austrian history. Klimt's golden world of Art Nouveau shimmer, richness, and elegance reflects the last brilliance of Imperial imperviousness; Schiele's austere Expressionist terrain maps out the collective *Angst* of prewar society. When we compare the two artists' renditions of similar motifs we immediately become aware of drastically different perceptions: Klimt's trees, for example (Pls. 9 and 10) are densely grouped, their trunks articulating an unusually low horizon line, their branches studding the entire upper two-thirds of the picture space with a mosaic of a thousand throbbing leaves. Schiele's autumnal tree (Pl. 1) stands alone silhouetted against the vastness of nature, its slender trunk anthropomorphically fragile as it leans toward a stake for support. The eternal recurrence promised by Klimt's plethora of nature is seen by his younger contemporary as an existential burden in a world of the nil. Klimt's society lady (Pl. 4) radiates confidence and self-esteem as opposed to Schiele's empathetic portrait of his father-in-law (Pl. 48), who sits abjectly, weighted down by large limbs and private thoughts. At times tender, the Expressionist artist grasps for phenomenological reassurance by isolating village buildings (Pls. 33, 34, and 36) or bridges (Pls. 37 and 38) and by singling out humble earthenware jugs and bowls (Pl. 56). The older artist still believes in decoration as a definer of environment (Pls. 18, 19, 27, 46, and 52); the younger often strips his subjects of their surroundings (Pls. 23, 24, 26, 32, 42, and 44), emphasizing the pathos of their vulnerability—a vulnerability so keenly felt by him that he voluntarily shares it in his *Self-Portrait as St. Sebastian* (Pl. 40). Their portraits of two children sum up the two epochs represented by Klimt and Schiele. Stubbornly Klimt clung to his vision of a fecund world in perpetual bloom and regeneration: his *Portrait of Mäda Primavesi* (Pl. 30) is confidently charged with ornamental and symbolic urgency. With equal determination Schiele sheared away the nineteenth-century façade of beauty to expose, in his portrait of a young street girl (Pl. 22), the grim specter of a child's psyche moored in modern uncertainty. Viewed side by side, these two artists, who were collected by Dr. Kallir in tandem, present the cultural chronology that led to the Austro-Hungarian explosion of 1914 and World War I. Such art, such epochs, such confrontations would never be possible again.

IF PART of Dr. Kallir's self-imposed mission (he also maintained an exhaustive documentation of the history of aeronautics) was to acquaint the world-at-large with Viennese art, an important element in his calling was the fact that he himself embodied the best Austria could export. From the luminous twinkle of his inquiring blue eyes and the lilt of his deep, musical voice to his compassion for others and the strongly held convictions that animated his conduct and his career, he carried the world of probing Viennese humanism within him. His Galerie St. Etienne on West 57th Street, named in honor of Vienna's renowned cathedral, served as a constant and fascinating mirror for the passions of his searching mind and the discoveries of his aesthetic eye. Open to past and contemporary styles, to sophisticated and naïve art, he was a reliable promoter of the old and innovative impresario of the new. Unknown, untried artists (he gave the first solo exhibition to Grandma Moses) could approach him with portfolios of their work and receive serious and kindly attention. Not only museum officials but beginning collectors could rely on discreet, astute guidance from him. In spite of his demanding exhibition schedule (from Kollwitz to American Primitives to Contemporary Yugoslavs in a few months), publication projects (a Gerstl oeuvre catalogue, the meticulously produced facsimile of a Schiele sketchbook), and frequent European travel, Dr. Kallir's door was always open.

Thus it was that a timid inquiry sent to him from a graduate student in art history at the University of California at Berkeley was answered copiously, by return mail, and with an airmail stamp! The year was 1962 and the letter of inquiry to the Galerie St. Etienne contained some questions I had concerning the whereabouts of certàin self-portraits by Egon Schiele. The generous cooperation and photographic aid given by Dr. Kallir and his knowledgeable secretary, Hildegard Bachert, greatly enhanced my master's thesis on Schiele, and when Ph.D. studies at Columbia University led me to New York in the fall of 1964, it was the IRT subway and not an airmail stamp that brought me into frequent personal contact with the guru of Austrian art. He was quick to impress upon me that to master Schiele, I must master the German language . . . and European geography. How they laughed at the Galerie St. Etienne when, one day, hopeful that I had discovered "common themes" in Hodler and Schiele—both of whom favored painting figures of monklike men and solemn virgins—I telephoned in desperation to ask who the third person was in a painting by Hodler referred to by Schiele as the *Mönch, Jungfrau und Eiger*. My attention was swiftly directed to Swiss mountain names. For years afterward Dr. Kallir delighted in quizzing me as to when I was going to climb the Eiger.

DURING the next ten years I spent every summer in Vienna, interviewing Schiele's relatives and friends, and although my command of the German language and Viennese dialect did progress accordingly, there were occasional setbacks, usually hinging on the incomprehensibility of a single word. The following linguistic impasse, reported back "home" to the Galerie St. Etienne, was one of Dr. Kallir's favorites. Like him, I made the pilgrimage one summer to the small village of Neulengbach, where Schiele had been imprisoned for twenty-six days during the spring of 1912. After some persistent searching, I located and photographed the actual prison cell where, some sixty years earlier, the artist had produced some of the most eloquent images of his career. It was thrilling to match up the watercolor views he had made of his prison cell and the dismal corridor just outside with the real sites (then in a state of great decay but now refurbished by the Austrian government). The result of this happy find was my first book, *Schiele in Prison*. But the village was not so kind to me in my attempt to find a specimen of *Judenkirsche*—the winter cherry plant which Schiele had joyously included in several of his Neulengbach pictures. No matter where or how many times I asked, no one in Neulengbach seemed to recognize or have any knowledge of the possible whereabouts of this indigenous but apparently rare plant. *"Keine Juden Kirche hier,"* I was told emphatically by one and all. Could it have been my American accent, Dr. Kallir theorized later with amusement, that led the villagers to believe I was asking directions to a "Jewish church"? Or, more likely, gleeful native contrariness, he added to console me.

Such was the complicated, many-sided, amazingly rich but sometimes frustratingly obdurate terrain, the nuances of which Dr. Kallir, Ambassador-at-Large for Austrian Art, helped me to comprehend over a precious sixteen years of friendship.

Figure 1. Installation of first Schiele exhibition at the Neue Galerie. Shown on the right wall are *The Bridge,* *Portrait of an Old Man,* and *Embrace.*

Kallir, Klimt and Schiele

by Jane Kallir

In THE AUTUMN of 1939, several days after his arrival in the United States, Dr. Otto Kallir was scurrying about Manhattan in search of office space. Many months earlier, he had left his Neue Galerie in Vienna, driven out by the Nazi *Anschluss,* to found the Galerie St. Etienne in Paris. Now it was his intention to open a branch in America. As things turned out, return to Paris was soon as impossible as return to Vienna, and the Galerie St. Etienne in New York became Dr. Kallir's base for the rest of his life.

Kallir had brought with him countless European art treasures of the nineteenth and twentieth centuries, many of which were virtually unknown in the United States. One of the shows which he organized during his first year in New York was entitled "Saved from Europe," and included works by masters such as Picasso, Utrillo, Signac, and Toulouse-Lautrec. Also exhibited were the works of two obscure Austrians, Gustav Klimt and Egon Schiele. The *New York Herald Tribune* observed dryly: "A good many of the canvases by reputable Europeans are definitely worth saving from Europe, whence they have recently come to this country. We are not so sure, however, that the reception here to the paintings of Schiele and Klimt will be all that may be expected for them. It is difficult to awaken enthusiasm at this time for artists so little known and appreciated here and for many years passed from the contemporary scene in Europe."[1]

In the spring of 1978, Dr. Kallir was no longer mounting regularly scheduled exhibitions, and his face showed a weariness caused by several years of intermittent illness. Nevertheless, he was still capable of vibrant bursts of enthusiasm if tempted by an appealing proposal. Such was his reaction when, late one afternoon, he received a call from J. Carter Brown, Director of the National Gallery of Art in Washington, D.C. Mr. Brown was putting the finishing touches to the Museum's new East Building, and wondered whether a painting, Gustav Klimt's *Baby* (Pl. 52), which he had long admired, might be available for the opening. It was. Although Dr. Kallir passed away before the end of that year, he had lived to see a Klimt painting acquired by the official state museum of his adopted land. It had, indeed, been "difficult to awaken enthusiasm" for the art of Klimt and Schiele in America, but Otto Kallir had succeeded.

It is often said that success has many friends, while failure stands alone. For many years, my grandfather was more or less alone in championing the work of his compatriots Klimt and

Schiele in the United States. During the last decades, however, growing recognition has considerably swollen the ranks of interested persons. The current wave of appreciation for the twilight years of the Austro-Hungarian Empire finds countless outlets: reprints of literary works, new historical and cultural studies, films of both a documentary and dramatic nature, television shows, exhibitions, posters, fabrics, and furniture. . . . The scope of these endeavors is amazing. One might easily interpret this surge of activity as a spontaneous development if one is unaware of the many years of painstaking work which went into cultivating the awareness that now seems to blossom forth so naturally. Undeniably, changes in the cultural atmosphere have contributed to the current popularity of Viennese art. However, such changes require a catalyst if they are to assume a definite direction. Dr. Kallir, by tirelessly laying the groundwork through his exhibitions and writings, was this catalyst.

A Revisionist Approach

Until recently, there was little room for Austrian art in America's cultural heritage. Following World War II, the close alliance of modern American painting with the French avant-garde rendered other national movements second-rate.[2] Critics postulated that the path of art-historical evolution led like an invisible thread from prewar Paris to postwar New York. The modernist impulse resurfaced here in Abstract Expressionism, and grew inexorably more abstract. Within this context, the figurative art of the two Austrians Gustav Klimt and Egon Schiele had little relevance. By the 1960s, however, things had begun to change.

Discussing Klimt and Schiele during this pivotal decade, journalists and scholars were quick to point out their relationship to the contemporary art scene. Klimt expert Johannes Dobai noted that a reevaluation of the whole Art Nouveau period had led to the rediscovery of Gustav Klimt. Thomas M. Messer, Director of the Solomon R. Guggenheim Museum, commented that Klimt's work, "seemingly old fashioned a generation ago, has moved toward the center of modern perception," and attributed this turnabout to "a readjustment of our critical sensibilities." Klimt had remained obscure, he stated, because "we failed to look, or at least, because we were incapable of seeing while our attention was focused in other directions."[3] Appreciation of the figurative element in art had been renewed. Critics observed that there was an affinity between current neo-representational work and the nudes of Egon Schiele.[4] Herschel Chipp, who had organized an important exhibition of Austrian art on the West Coast, felt a reexamination of the human body as an expressive force to be imminent, and saw the basis for this in the emotional aspects of Abstract Expressionism. Referring to Viennese Expressionism, he contended that "the themes of this movement, anxieties, suffering of physical and psychic origin, morbid speculation on death, and an overt sexuality, certainly have a special appeal in American culture today." He felt that this appeal, as much as anything, had stimulated interest in Schiele and Klimt.[5]

Laying the Groundwork

It is perhaps no coincidence that works by both Schiele and Klimt received their first extensive American exposure during the 1960s. This newly kindled appreciation prompted

16

Dr. Kallir to publish an oeuvre catalogue of Schiele's graphic work in 1970 as a complement to his catalogue of the paintings, which had been reissued in 1966.[6] In 1965, the Guggenheim Museum mounted the most extensive exhibition of works by Klimt and Schiele ever seen in the United States. It was the second of two ground-breaking collaborations between Otto Kallir and Thomas Messer. The first, a Schiele exhibition, had taken place five years earlier, when Messer was still Director of the Institute of Contemporary Art in Boston. After one month in Boston, the show moved on to Kallir's New York gallery. Through the spring of 1961, it traveled to three other American cities: Louisville, Pittsburgh, and Minneapolis.

Two seminal exhibitions in the late 1950s paved the way for the triumphs of the 60s. In 1959, the first Klimt show ever held in the United States opened at the Galerie St. Etienne. Newspaper critics could hardly believe that a one-man exhibition had never before taken place, for they already felt quite at home with Klimt.[7] The ease with which Klimt won acceptance was attributed to two important museum acquisitions.[8] In 1957, Kallir had sold the Museum of Modern Art its first Klimt, *The Park* (Pl. 9). The year before, he had donated *Pear Tree* (Pl. 10) to the Fogg Art Museum at Harvard University.

In 1957, the Galerie St. Etienne had its first successful Schiele exhibition. Like the Klimt show, it was preceded by a milestone museum purchase. Three years earlier, the Minneapolis Institute of Arts had become the first museum in the country to own an oil painting by Egon Schiele, his *Portrait of the Painter Paris von Gütersloh* (Pl. 58). This development was considered significant enough to be given national news coverage.[9]

At the time, Dr. Kallir believed that these three major paintings, which he donated or sold for nominal sums, would do more good in museums than they would at his gallery. In this he was right, though he was mistaken when he said he would never be able to sell them for anything near their true value. Such pessimism is understandable when one realizes that, before then, Kallir's efforts to interest America in Klimt and Schiele had not been very fruitful. The first American Schiele show, which took place in 1941, had been met with indifference, as had the second one in 1948. Works by Klimt and Schiele which Kallir included in his group shows of the forties and fifties were apt to be overlooked. Nonetheless, he persevered. As the Galerie St. Etienne approached its twentieth anniversary, his policy of repeatedly presenting the art of Austrian masters began to produce results.

What Took So Long?

Once Klimt and Schiele had begun to attract attention, there was a certain amount of speculation as to why recognition had taken so long. One frequently advanced explanation was that the erotic element, especially in Schiele's work, had been considered objectionable.[10] Dr. Kallir, in selecting pieces for exhibition in the forties and fifties, took into account the prevailing moral standards. As late as 1960, Thomas Messer was able to write in the catalogue for the Boston show: "Since we did not wish to invite discussion which would be artistically irrelevant, we avoided subjects that might be considered extreme."[11] Perhaps because their contents were deliberately subdued, Schiele exhibitions in the United States never provoked any moral outrage. On the contrary. When Schiele's work was first seen in New York, it was said that "his style . . . shows little . . . penetration, and is definitely ascribable to the decorative category."[12] Such sentiments, surprising in view of the passionate intensity we now recognize in Schiele's art, were repeated in reviews of the 1948 show.[13]

Whatever the effect of the erotic aspect had been previously, in the changing climate of the 1960s it was a decided plus. Kallir and Messer no longer needed to worry about being accused of spreading pornography, for their 1960 show actually drew criticism for its limitation of overtly sexual material.[14] This clamour for more nudes was heard again in response to the Guggenheim exhibition.[15] The new attitude toward sex was exemplified by an illustrated magazine piece that eagerly promised to introduce its readers to "the strange erotic world of Egon Schiele."[16] Alessandra Comini's monographs on Klimt and Schiele, which did much to popularize their work in the 1970s, displayed uninhibited candor.[17]

There were, then, more serious obstacles to the recognition of Schiele and Klimt than the prurient undertones in their art. One was the fact that, quite literally, neither artist was around to defend himself. Klimt and Schiele, who had both died in 1918, faced some of their keenest competition from a fellow Austrian, Oskar Kokoschka. Kokoschka had the advantage of being alive, and was widely acknowledged as Austria's leading Expressionist.[18] He had, furthermore, achieved international recognition through exposure in Germany, rather than in his native land. Basically, Expressionism was viewed as a German movement, and its Austrian counterpart was ignored.[19]

Further difficulties were created for Klimt and Schiele by Austrian government policy, which restricted the international availability of their work. In the wake of World War II, the Austrians had become increasingly protective of their art treasures. The period of German domination, and the narrow margin with which Austria escaped absorption by the Soviet bloc, heightened national cultural consciousness. Because many important paintings had been lost or destroyed in the Nazi holocaust,[20] the government, anxious to preserve what remained, imposed strict export controls. The state museums, which jointly have the largest collection of Klimt and Schiele anywhere, became increasingly nervous about lending. Although they were willing to make paintings available for major exhibitions, the fragility of certain items made it dangerous for them to travel any great distance. Therefore, the Guggenheim Museum was unable to exhibit Klimt's most famous pieces. In 1959, the Galerie St. Etienne actually supplemented the original paintings in its Klimt show with framed reproductions. It is ironic that, while Klimt is best loved for his "gold" paintings, only two have ever been seen in the United States.[21]

Before these limitations were imposed, a surprising number of works by Klimt and Schiele had made their way to America. During the Nazi years, Klimt, Schiele, and many other artists were banned as "degenerate." In Germany, avant-garde art was rounded up and sent on a traveling exhibition as a warning to any who might challenge the Führer's taste. Then it was shipped abroad and sold. The Austrians made no similar effort to dispose of the art outlawed by Hitler. Nonetheless, "degenerate" works could not be exhibited, and emigrating refugees were not prohibited from taking them along. Thus the cultural policies of the Nazis encouraged the spread of works by Klimt and Schiele throughout the world.

Kallir in Vienna

When Otto Kallir left Vienna in 1938, his Neue Galerie had acquired an enviable reputation for showing a broad range of art. One of his overriding interests had, for many years, been the work of Egon Schiele. The basis for all future Schiele scholarship, including Kallir's 1966 book, was established by his 1930 catalogue of the artist's paintings.[22] In 1928, Kallir arranged one of the most extensive Schiele shows ever held (eighty-three oils) at the Hagenbund, an artists' organization which had exhibited Schiele during his lifetime. The first one-man show after Schiele's death had also been organized by Kallir. A first in more ways than one, this 1923 exhibition inaugurated the Neue Galerie (Fig. 1).

Kallir's fascination with Schiele had begun even before he opened his gallery. He had started his career in the arts as a publisher of limited-edition original graphics. When he learned of an unsold edition of Schiele etchings and lithographs, he longed to assume responsibility for their distribution. However, the financial requirements of the undertaking made it impossible for him to act immediately. It was not until 1921 that, under the auspices of the Rikola Verlag, he was able to purchase the prints and issue them in portfolio form.[23]

Journalist Max Roden can be credited with introducing Otto Kallir to Schiele's work. World War I was still raging, and Kallir, an officer in the Imperial Army, never dreamed that he would one day own an art gallery. Roden told him of a young artist, a fellow soldier, who was desperately in need of money. This chap, he said, was willing to make portrait sketches for 100 Kronen (then the equivalent of roughly $20.00). For this fee, the sitter would be offered a choice of three drawings: two in black and white, and one with watercolor. The young Kallir was tempted, but his father, a well-known attorney, advised against such extravagance. Kallir always regretted this lost opportunity to have his portrait drawn by Egon Schiele.

He would not twice turn down such a chance. A short time later, still in the face of opposition from his family, Kallir made his first real art purchase. After being discharged from the army, he used his final pay to acquire a group of about fifty Klimt drawings. These pieces contributed greatly to the initial stock of the Neue Galerie and later the Galerie St. Etienne. Even at Dr. Kallir's death, the collection had not been entirely exhausted.

Although today the discouragement which Kallir received from his father seems unwarranted, there was good reason for concern. The Austrian political and economic plight made expenditures for art seem quite frivolous. In 1918, the end of World War I and that of the Empire collided with a brutal impact. As the soldiers slowly returned from the Front, it became clear to them that Austria's defeat had been suffered less on the battlefield than at home. Nowhere was the situation more desperate than in Vienna. Cut off from the direct sources of food available to rural communities, the city starved. Long bread lines were a common sight, and a black market developed to provide food and fuel to those who could pay the price. As the supply of coal for heating dwindled, the incidence of the deadly Spanish Flu reached epidemic proportions. Two of its victims were Egon Schiele and his wife, Edith, who died in October, 1918. Gustav Klimt had succumbed several months earlier to the aftereffects of a stroke.

Klimt and Schiele: Their Lives

Over half a century has passed since the deaths of Klimt and Schiele. Looking back now, vision blurred by the passage of time, it may initially be difficult to perceive any but the most superficial connection between these two Viennese painters. In Klimt we sense the dying breaths of the nineteenth century, the decadent demise of a decadent movement: Art Nouveau. Schiele could be viewed as his opposite, innovator of a rugged Expressionist idiom.[24] Nonetheless, in the hothouse environment of Vienna, even such seemingly disparate aesthetic impulses show evidence of common roots.

If Klimt had followed the path suggested by his early career, it might be reasonable to label him a conservative. Born in 1862, Klimt studied art in an era dominated by the painter Hans Makart. The Makart phenomenon, based on grandiose portrayals of nudes in overblown historical settings, had taken Vienna by storm, influencing everything from hats to parlor furnishings. The height of Makart's achievement was a five-hour-long festival parade (*Festzug*) arranged to celebrate the Emperor's silver wedding anniversary. The young Klimt no doubt considered himself privileged to share in the preparations for this gala event, which involved extensive copying of historical motifs.

Shortly after completing his education, Klimt began to receive important public commissions. Together with his brother Ernst and painter Franz Matsch, he created ceiling paintings for one of Empress Elizabeth's bedrooms and for the newly constructed Burgtheater. In 1888, his contributions to the theater decorations earned him a gold service cross from the Emperor. When, two years later, the team of Klimt, Matsch, and Klimt was asked to finish a project in the Kunsthistorisches Museum begun by Makart before his death, Gustav Klimt's position as Makart's heir was assured.

However, a different fate awaited him. After his brother's death in 1892, Klimt's working relationship with Matsch began to deteriorate. In 1894, the two painters received a commission that was to mark a turning point for Klimt: the ceiling paintings for the Great Hall at the University of Vienna.

In all of Vienna there was, at this time, only one place where artists could exhibit their work. The Künstlerhaus, founded in 1861, had gained prominence during the Makart era. This conservative institution, of which Klimt was a member, dominated the Viennese art scene. In April, 1897, a group of the younger artists organized a new society, with Klimt as president, to represent more modern views within the existing framework. Initially, there was no plan for an all-out break. However, when the executive committee of the Künstlerhaus voted to censure the rebels, the Secession as an independent entity was born.

Although the Secession has been described as a revolutionary force, it was never in true cultural exile. The desire to retain ties with the establishment led the Secession to recruit "respectable" older members such as painter Rudolf Alt and architect Otto Wagner. Furthermore, the Secessionists had little trouble gathering financial and political support. Scarcely a year and a half after leaving the Künstlerhaus, they had built their own exhibition hall.

There it was that, in March, 1900, Klimt exhibited *Philosophy* (Novotny/Dobai 105), the

Figure 2. Gustav Klimt. *Portrait of Fritza Riedler.* 1906. (Novotny/Dobai 143.)
Oesterreichische Galerie, Vienna.

first of his three paintings for the University of Vienna. A violent public outcry was engendered by the picture's undraped nudes, which cavorted freely without any historical context. The other two University paintings, *Medicine* (Novotny/Dobai 112) and *Jurisprudence* (Novotny/Dobai 128), shown in 1901 and 1903 respectively, elicited similar reactions. In spite of these protests, the Ministry of Education approved all three canvases. It was left to Klimt, harassed by the criticism, to renounce the commission and repay the advance he had received.

The early years of this century must have been unpleasant for Klimt. Not only was he bombarded by attacks on his University paintings, he was also having problems with his fellow artists. Klimt was a firm believer, with Josef Hoffmann and Koloman Moser, in the

Gesamtkunstwerk. This concept, fostered by the Wiener Werkstätte which Hoffmann and Moser founded, promoted an alliance of the fine and applied arts in a total aesthetic environment. This emphasis on utilitarian design applications angered the easel painters in the Secession. In 1905, the *Klimt-Gruppe* went off on its own, leaving the Secession's most important asset—its building—in the hands of the more conservative artists.

So it happened that, within less than ten years, Klimt had twice broken with established institutions. He was, nevertheless, a well-known and admired artist. It is not surprising, then, that when Egon Schiele came to Vienna in 1906 to study at the Academy of Art, he was overwhelmed by Klimt's style. By 1907, Schiele had mustered the courage to seek out the older artist for advice. Klimt was quite taken with the work of this precocious seventeen-year-old. When Schiele later suggested that they exchange drawings, Klimt remarked that Schiele would be getting the raw end of the deal in such a trade. "You draw better than I do anyway," he reportedly said.[25] Still, Klimt acquired Schiele's drawings both through trade and purchase. He also tried to help Schiele by introducing him to wealthy collectors.

In 1908 and 1909, Klimt organized two exhibitions that were called simply Kunstschau (art show). He and his associates had regrouped in an elaborate prefabricated structure designed by Hoffmann. Here they hoped to serve the twin purposes of promulgating the *Gesamtkunstwerk* and introducing Vienna to avant-garde art from all over Europe. Schiele, upon Klimt's invitation, contributed four paintings to the second of these exhibitions.

Around the time of the Kunstschau 1909, Schiele took a step that mimicked Klimt's rebellions in form though not in substance. If the Künstlerhaus was one bastion of conservative authority in Vienna, the Academy of Art was the other. Schiele's growing discomfort there finally caused him to drop out in the spring of 1909. As Klimt had done before him, he attempted to found a society based on his principles: the *Neukunstgruppe.* Schiele's group exhibited together several times, and some of its members did eventually achieve a certain degree of renown. However, the impact of this student protest on the world at large was negligible, whereas its personal consequences for Schiele were enormous. The grudging financial support he had so far received from his family was withdrawn, initiating a long period of deprivation.

Klimt, unlike Schiele, never lacked material comforts, and was, in fact, the darling of wealthy society ladies. Still, he did feel keenly the barbs hurled at him by less liberal factions. Indeed, Vienna has acquired quite a reputation for being a vicious mother who eats her young alive. Noting that Klimt's controversial *Philosophy* was awarded the *Grand Prix* at the Exposition Universelle in Paris, Felix Salten commented: "One can tell that Klimt is a Viennese from the fact that he is honored throughout the world and attacked only in Vienna."[26]

Schiele, too, harbored feelings of bitterness toward the Imperial capital. "I would like to leave Vienna as soon as possible," he wrote his friend Anton Peschka. "How ugly everything is here. Everyone is full of envy and behaves dishonestly toward me. There is falsehood in the eyes of former colleagues. Vienna is full of shadow. A black city. I want to be alone."[27]

Schiele's desire for a place where he could work undisturbed led him, in 1911, to Krumau, his mother's home town. The appearance of the village, its houses tightly packed on a narrow peninsula, enthralled him. He hoped that he had at last found a peaceful refuge, but it was not to be. His cohabitation with model Wally Neuzil, and his practice of asking young girls to pose for him, angered the staid villagers, and he was forced to leave.

The citizens of Neulengbach, where he settled next, were even less receptive to his bohemian ways. A misunderstanding concerning the daughter of a retired naval officer led to the artist's arrest. After twenty-one days in jail awaiting trial, he received a minimal sentence for disseminating "obscene" drawings. The period in prison, and the experience of seeing the judge burn one of his drawings, wounded Schiele deeply.

Scandals instigated by the 'prurient' nature of his work dogged Klimt as well as Schiele. It has already been noted that the impetus of the attacks on the University paintings was their overt sexual content. Klimt's poster for the first Secession exhibition stimulated similar protests. Public opinion forced Klimt to cover the male genitalia visible in the original design with Art Nouveau weeds. Klimt's twenty-year relationship with his mistress, Emilie Flöge, flew in the face of the prevailing behavioral code. His conduct and his tendency toward the risqué did not, however, subject Klimt to the kind of persecution faced by Schiele.

After the Neulengbach incident, Schiele decided that life in Vienna might after all have its advantages. He found a studio in one of the city's outlying districts, and turned his full attention to his painting. Although he was still in a state of depression following the prison ordeal, Schiele's career was beginning to pick up. He was being asked to contribute to group shows with a certain degree of regularity. In 1913, he had three one-man exhibitions: typically, not in Austria but in Germany.

About that time, Schiele began a flirtation that was to have far-reaching results. Two sisters, Adele and Edith Harms, who lived across the street, caught his eye. At first he seemed to favor both women equally, but his interest eventually focused on Edith. After being drafted into the army in May 1915, he hastily married her before reporting for duty.

Schiele did not take well to military life, and was terrified of being sent to the Front. Fortunately, he was reclassified as fit only for limited service. In spite of his frequent complaints, Schiele's lot was better than that of most. When stationed in Vienna, he was allowed to return home during his free time, thereby permitting him to continue painting. In addition to a number of substantial oils, he executed penetrating watercolor and pencil studies of Austrian officers and Russian prisoners of war (Pl. 47).

The last year of Schiele's life, 1918, was also the year of his first real success. In March his work was featured in the Secession's forty-ninth exhibition, for which he designed the poster. Not only was the show well received by the press, but, for the first time, he sold enough to relieve his financial worries.

The new avant-garde—Expressionism—had achieved recognition in the house of the old avant-garde—the Secession. As if to complete a symbolic circle, Klimt, former leader of the Secession, had in 1917 been awarded an honorary professorship at that center of reaction, the Vienna Academy of Art. The chain of succession, from Makart to Klimt to Schiele, was confirmed.

Their Art

Art historian Johannes Dobai has commented that "with the Viennese, . . . anxiety, . . . the fruit of an overripe culture, . . . reveals itself in an erotic frenzy springing from a feeling of emptiness. . . . Wanting to fill this emptiness, Klimt filled his bare canvases with his Art Nouveau experiments."[28] Schiele, one could add, jumped into the void.

If Klimt was preoccupied with the problem of filling space, it must soon have become evident that he would have to develop two solutions: one for his landscapes, the other for portraits. While nature presents a continuous expanse of form and texture, two very different entities must be merged when one places a human being in space.

Klimt's *horror vacui* was assuaged by the interpretation of nature as unbroken pattern. In *The Park, Pear Tree,* and *Island in the Attersee* (Pls. 9, 10, and 8), all painted before 1910, the entire space has been filled with an all-encompassing design. Jewel-like foliage and shimmering water overwhelm these canvases, subordinating representational content to the general flow. The characteristic square format, by its equal emphasis of each edge, facilitates interpretation of the picture plane as a compositional entity divorced from reality. These early landscapes are some of the artist's most radical works. Klimt's treatment of nature would become less extreme as he aged.

Figures in an environment presented a different kind of challenge. One solution, which would be developed in the gold paintings of the early 1900s, was the use of geometric structures. This device is foreshadowed in a painting of circa 1890, *Two Girls with Oleander* (Pl. 2). The abstract background, provided here by the warm yellow architectural masses, and the attention to details such as floral growth, textile design, and ornamental carving, would reappear in the artist's later portraits (Figs. 2 and 3). Another device employed by Klimt was the dispersal of human bodies in organic patterns. In his 1898 canvas *Moving Water* (Pl. 7), nude women float like limp seaweed in the water. By 1907 or 1908, in *Hope II* (Pl. 18), Klimt had arrived at the solution of intertwining human and decorative forms, using the mottled background as an abstract foil for his symbolic structure.

Klimt evolved technical as well as compositional methods to fill his canvases, using the interplay of color and brushstroke to suggest substance where he perceived a vacuum. By overlapping and mingling multicolored dabs of pigment in his landscapes (Pls. 8, 10, and 11), he achieved both chromatic and textural unity. In *Woman with Fur Collar* (Pl. 4), the modulation of red tones, from the brownish depths of the collar to the pink highlights on the face, creates a monochromatic impression. As the boundaries between figure and ground blur, the tension between two inherently disparate elements is eased.

The relationship between subject and background in Schiele's *Portrait of the Painter Zakovsek* (Pl. 23) is, by comparison, quite distinct. The coloration of Zakovsek's body clearly separates it from the empty surroundings in which it floats uneasily. The sitter leans at an angle, resting on a nonexistent chair, and his right elbow is propped on an invisible armrest. Unlike Klimt's fur-clad lady, so poised and obviously well-to-do, Zakovsek appears weary and dissipated, a ghostlike messenger from the void.

1910, the year in which Schiele painted his portrait of Zakovsek, marked a turning point for both painters. Klimt, perhaps influenced by a recent trip to Paris, abandoned his gold style. And Schiele, perhaps influenced by paintings he had seen at the Kunstschau of 1909, departed decisively from his earlier Klimtian style.

From his Art Nouveau experiments, Schiele retained a feeling for elegant line. How easily the style derived from Klimt could be turned to more expressive ends is demonstrated by a comparison of Schiele's *Girl in a Plaid Garment* (Pl. 15), done in 1909, and his *Standing Nude Girl* (Pl. 16), done about a year later. Some elements of the two works are very similar: the demure turning away of the head, the coy closed eyes, the bony angularity of elbows and shoulders. The composition of the earlier work is, however, influenced by Klimt, not only in its emphasis on pattern but also in its use of drapery to conceal the figure below the waist.[29] The positioning of the girl's hands and arms is purely decorative here, whereas in the other study these elements assume a psychological function. The girl moves the drapery to the side, exposing her crotch, and, in a gesture both sensual and modest, she folds her arms over her breasts. The tensely splayed fingers of the right hand are highlighted with watercolor. Schiele, with these simple means, has captured the essence of a young girl's awakening sexuality.

Technically speaking, the problem which confronted Schiele after 1910 was the union of color and line. Unlike Klimt, he preferred his paint thin, and (especially in his watercolors) enjoyed exploring the nuances that could be obtained with a single layer of pigment. In his *Portrait of Eduard Kosmak* (Pl. 26), he swirls the paint over the gnarled surface of a hand, allowing a puddle to accumulate on the knuckles, then recede, blending in a touch of purple while the paint is still wet. At the edge of the eyes, he pulls back, letting the thin outline of the iris rest in a penetrating hollow. As though to keep the paint from exploding, he outlines the figure with bold strokes of white.

Confining his paint within a linear structure was partly a residue of Schiele's experience with Art Nouveau geometry. His *Stein on the Danube II* (Pl. 36) is essentially a two-dimensional line composition. The windows, inserted like cut gems in the walls, recall the silver squares in the background of Klimt's *Portrait of Fritza Riedler* (Fig. 2). The clear delineation of shapes is, however, very different from Klimt's style of his later period. Klimt, filling in a grid on the roof of his *House in Garden* (Pl. 35), loses patience with the little lines and blurs them with hasty dabs. The lush foliage in this painting, which seems about to engulf the house, contrasts sharply with the neat strips of green in Schiele's "Stein." Klimt's application of paint, so thick and generous, is decidedly different from that of Schiele, whose color softly sinks into the canvas.

The most profound difference between Klimt and Schiele occurs in the emotional content of their work. Schiele not only digs deeply into the psychological depths of his sitters, but lays bare his own anguish in a plethora of self-portraits. The cockiness of his 1910 self-image (Pl. 25) gives way to the tired and somewhat battered Schiele we see in 1912 (Pl. 39). The 1914 *Self-Portrait as St. Sebastian* (Pl. 40) epitomizes the artist's use of line as an emotional force. The figure has been twisted and flattened unnaturally by the intensity of its suffering.

Klimt, on the other hand, rarely painted men, and his women, sometimes buried up to their necks in ornament, do not display very vibrant personalities. It may be hypothesized

Figure 3.
Gustav Klimt.
*Portrait of Friederike
Maria Beer.* 1916.
(Novotny/Dobai 196.)
Private collection.

that Klimt was fleeing confrontation with the self by his concentration on the opposite sex, and that the decorative treatment of the females in his paintings is also an avoidance tactic.

In any case, Klimt was frankly envious of the expressive power Schiele was able to generate.[30] Perhaps inspired by the younger artist's frontal portraits, he adopted a similar approach. However, as in his *Portrait of Mäda Primavesi* (Pl. 30), the impact is softened by a background strewn with blossoms and trinkets. Klimt's females, encased in elaborate design motifs, often acquire the facial penetration of porcelain dolls (Fig. 3). In paintings like *The Dancer* (Pl. 46), the ornamental patterns which clothe the model merge with those in her environment. The woman, in constrast to these busy surroundings, remains serene, looking into the distance with an almost catatonic expression.

In Schiele's portrait of his wife, Edith, (Pl. 44), we see a prototypical Klimt woman with all background detail stripped away. Only the pattern of the dress remains, and the numb, doll-like stare. Schiele's obsession here with the pattern of the garment might almost be considered a parody of his one-time mentor. Without the Klimtian decorative surround, the dress billows awkwardly, the arms hang limply, the feet protrude dumbly. The artist's pretty wife stares at us with all the intellectual awareness of a captured butterfly. The entire Klimt world has been turned inside out and we gape at its hollow core.

Unlike his portrait of Edith, Schiele's depiction of her father, *Portrait of an Old Man* (Pl. 48), is startling for its simplicity and emotional depth. Although we do not see the man's eyes, or even his entire face, the subtle eloquence of his pose conveys profound weariness and resignation. The colors are subdued, possibly to emphasize the grayness of old age. The sitter exists in a vacuum, and his angular pose harkens back to Zakovsek's, but the addition of a chair is a new, reassuring element.

In Schiele's earlier work, his lines had been lean, his forms reduced to patterns within which his powerful brushstroke could be free to wander. Gradually, his art had begun to take a more naturalistic direction. Already in his "St. Sebastian," he had supplemented the outline with frenetic cross-hatching. Similarly, red and green paint were used to give volume to the line in *Nude Girl Sitting on Orange Cloth* (Pl. 41), also executed in 1914. This return to plastic form and three-dimensional space continued to develop. His drawing style by 1917 employs line to suggest solidity (Pl. 53), and his use of paint now serves a more specifically anatomical function (Pls. 49 and 55). The settings for his portraits are more realistically described; as in the "Old Man," there are chairs (Pls. 51 and 58), and, in his last portraits, there are walls (Pl. 57). Moreover, Schiele's application of paint has become heavier. The manipulation of overlapping colors, long since mastered by Klimt, is adapted to expressive ends.

Schiele's unfinished *Portrait of the Painter Paris von Gütersloh* (Pl. 58) is evidence of the force inherent in the new technique. As in earlier portraits, we confront the sitter face to face. He stares at us wide-eyed, his lips set solemnly. The hands, always a key element for Schiele, are raised, the fingers a-tremble. This quivering energy is reflected in the paint surface of the entire canvas. The white shirt conceals a wealth of other colors, and the bright background is composed of frenzied strokes. The blue of Gütersloh's tie vibrates in juxtaposition with the complementary orange.

Klimt's development in the last years of his life is more difficult to define concretely. The growth of his bright patterns remains unchecked in the unfinished canvas *Baby* (Pl. 52). Klimt had always been attracted to triangular configurations: his Mäda Primavesi stood on one, and Elisabeth Bachofen-Echt (Novotny/Dobai 188) was posed in front of one. The baby, however, is consumed by a triangle. The decorative coverlet has forced the infant's head to the top of the canvas, and it seems that the little creature is about to disappear. There has been some theorizing that Klimt was on the verge of an Expressionistic breakthrough when he died, but such speculations can never be proven. With both Klimt and Schiele, the question of what might have been must remain unanswered.

Gustav Klimt:

A Chronology

1862 Born July 14, son of a gold engraver, in Baumgarten, a suburb of Vienna.

1876–1883 Studies at the Kunstgewerbeschule in Vienna.

1886–1892 With his brother Ernst (1864–1892) and Franz Matsch (1861–1942), Klimt paints ceiling pictures for the Burgtheater and the Kunsthistorisches Museum in Vienna. Member of the Künstlerhaus Association, Vienna (1891–1897).

1897 Co-founder and first president of the Vienna Secession.

1898 First exhibition of Secession. Often contributes designs to the periodical *Ver Sacrum.* Signs contract with Austrian government to paint panels of the three faculties, *Philosophy, Medicine,* and *Jurisprudence,* for auditorium of Vienna University. From now on spends summers mostly at the Attersee. Paints first landscapes. Uses gold and silver in several symbolic works.

1900 Participates in the Exposition Universelle in Paris and receives a prize for *Philosophy;* in Vienna the painting had caused a scandal earlier that year.

1902 *Beethoven Frieze* is exhibited at the Vienna Secession with Max Klinger's Beethoven monument.

1903 The Wiener Werkstätte is founded; Klimt exerts a strong influence. Major Klimt exhibition (80 works) at the Secession.

1905 Fed up with controversies surrounding the University pictures, Klimt returns honorarium. Leaves Secession with fourteen other artists. Commissioned by Josef Hoffmann, architect of the Stoclet House in Brussels, to design frieze for dining room (completed 1909, installed 1911).

1907 Meets and encourages the young artist Egon Schiele.

1908–1909 Organizes and exhibits in the Kunstschau (1908) and the Internationale Kunstschau (1909).

1910 Participates in the Esposizione Internazionale di Venezia and receives wide acclaim. Turns away from "golden" style.

1912 President, Bund österreichischer Künstler.

1913–1914 Participates in exhibitions in Budapest, Prague, Germany, and Rome.

1917 Honorary member of Academies in Vienna and Munich.

1918 On January 11, Gustav Klimt suffers a stroke; he dies on February 6 in Vienna.

Egon Schiele:

A Chronology

1890 Born on June 12, son of the railroad stationmaster in Tulln on the Danube, Austria.

1896–1900 Primary school in Tulln.

1902–1906 High school in Klosterneuburg near Vienna. His talent in drawing becomes predominant.

1906 In October, accepted at the Academy of Fine Arts in Vienna.

1907 Meets Gustav Klimt, who strongly influences his early work.

1908 Participates in his first public exhibition at Klosterneuburg.

1909 Leaves the Academy together with a group of progressive young artists; they found the *Neukunstgruppe*. Exhibits at the Internationale Kunstschau in Vienna. Meets art historian and critic Arthur Roessler, who encourages him.

1910 Schiele's own style emerges. Draws and paints many portraits and figural compositions which shock Vienna's conservative art circles.

1911 Rents a studio in Krumau, Bohemia, together with his model and friend Valerie Neuzil ("Wally"), but soon forced to leave. They move to Neulengbach, a hamlet near Vienna. Landscapes assume greater importance in his work.

1912 April 13–May 8, imprisoned on charges of alleged immorality. Moves to a studio in Vienna, which he retains until his death. Participates in the international Sonderbund exhibition in Cologne.

1913 Member of the Bund österreichischer Künstler. Increased exhibition activity, including one-man show at Galerie Goltz, Munich.

1914 Participates in exhibitions in Germany, Rome, Paris, Brussels; one-man show in Vienna.

1915 Marries Edith Harms. Inducted into the Austrian army, and after basic training is sent back to the vicinity of Vienna for guard duty and clerical work.

1916 The German periodical *Die Aktion* devotes a special issue to Schiele.

1917 Assigned to duty in Vienna and allowed to devote much time to painting. Participates in exhibitions in Munich, Amsterdam, and Scandinavia.

1918 In March, comprehensive exhibition at the Secession in Vienna is first great success. October 28, Edith Schiele dies of the Spanish Flu. On October 31, the day of her funeral, Egon Schiele also succumbs to the illness.

The Plates

Plate 2. Gustav Klimt. *Two Girls with Oleander*. Ca. 1890–92.

Plate 3. Gustav Klimt. *Seated Lady.* Ca. 1900.

Plate 4. Gustav Klimt.
Woman with Fur Collar.
Ca. 1897–98.

Plate 5. Gustav Klimt. *Portrait of a Woman in Profile.* 1897–98.

Plate 6. Gustav Klimt. *Seated Woman with Hat and Veil.* 1897–98.

Plate 7. Gustav Klimt. *Moving Water*. 1898.

Plate 8. Gustav Klimt. *Island in the Attersee.* Ca. 1901.

Plate 9. Gustav Klimt. *The Park*. Before 1910.

Plate 10. Gustav Klimt. *Pear Tree.* 1903, later worked over.

Plate 11. Gustav Klimt. *Orchard (Garden Landscape)*. Before 1910.

Plate 12. Egon Schiele. *Field of Flowers*. 1910.

Plate 13. Gustav Klimt. *Portrait of a Lady in Profile.* 1904–5.

Plate 14.
Gustav Klimt.
*Woman with Red
Hair.* 1908.

Plate 15. Egon Schiele.
Girl in a Plaid Garment.
Ca. 1909.

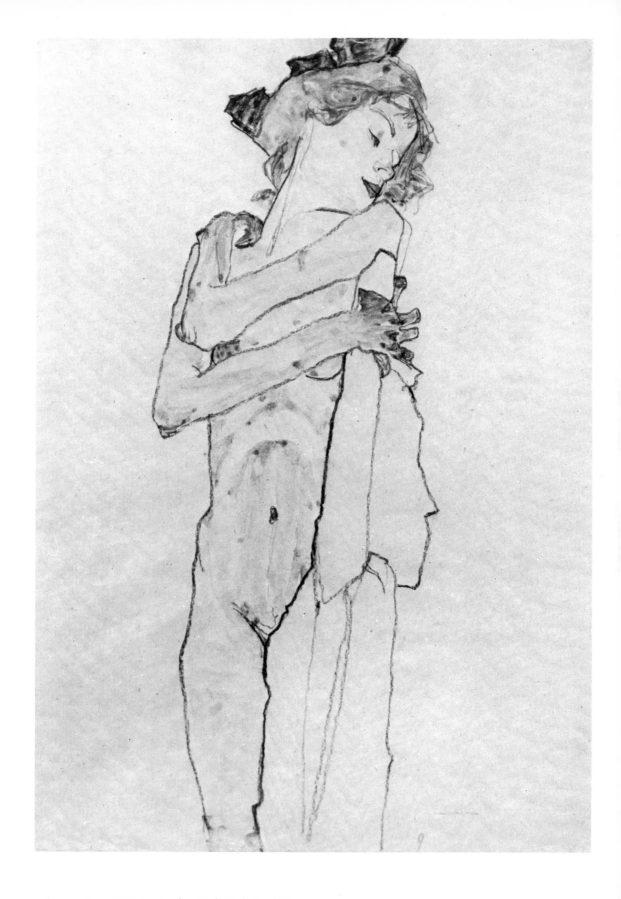

Plate 16. Egon Schiele. *Standing Nude Girl.* Ca. 1910.

Plate 17. Gustav Klimt. *Three Courtesans*. Ca. 1908.

Plate 18. Gustav Klimt. *Hope II (Vision; Fertility; Legend)*. 1907–8.

Plate 19. Gustav Klimt. *Lady with a Fan.* 1903–4.

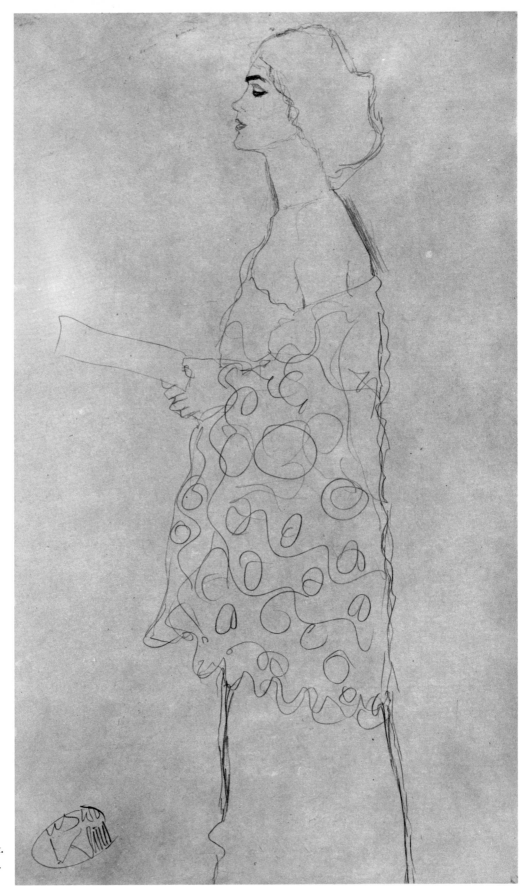

Plate 20. Gustav Klimt.
Standing Lady in Profile.
Ca. 1908.

Plate 21. Gustav Klimt. *Seated Woman.* Ca. 1914.

Plate 22.
Egon Schiele.
*Proletarian Girl
in Black.* 1910.

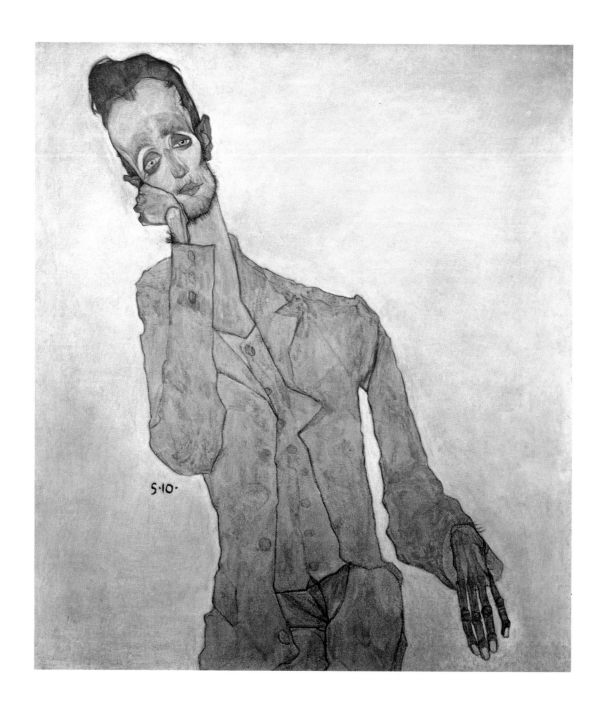

Plate 23. Egon Schiele. *Portrait of the Painter Zakovsek.* 1910.

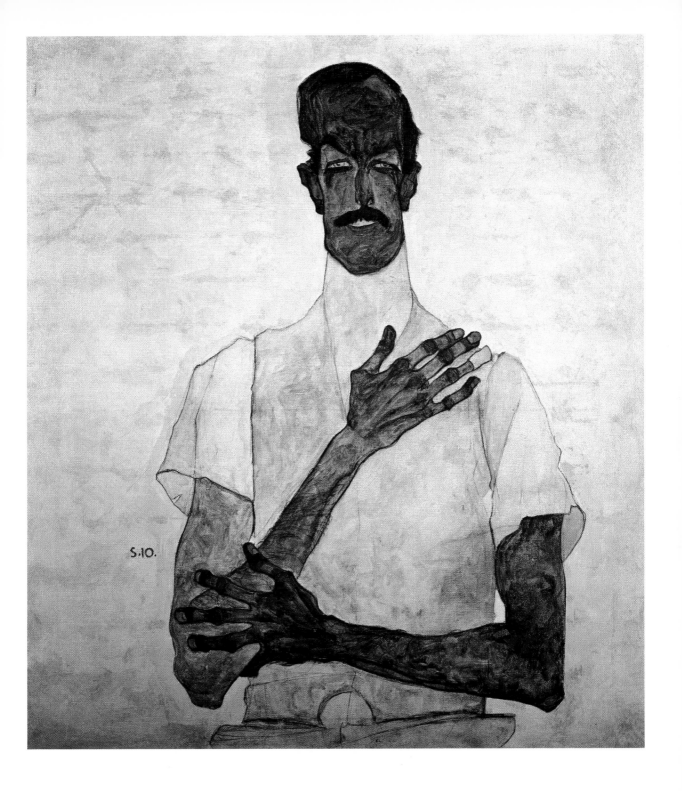

Plate 24. Egon Schiele. *Portrait of Dr. von Graff.* 1910.

SCHIELE 10.

Plate 26. Egon Schiele. *Portrait of Eduard Kosmak.* 1910.

Plate 25. Egon Schiele. *Self-Portrait, Standing.* 1910.

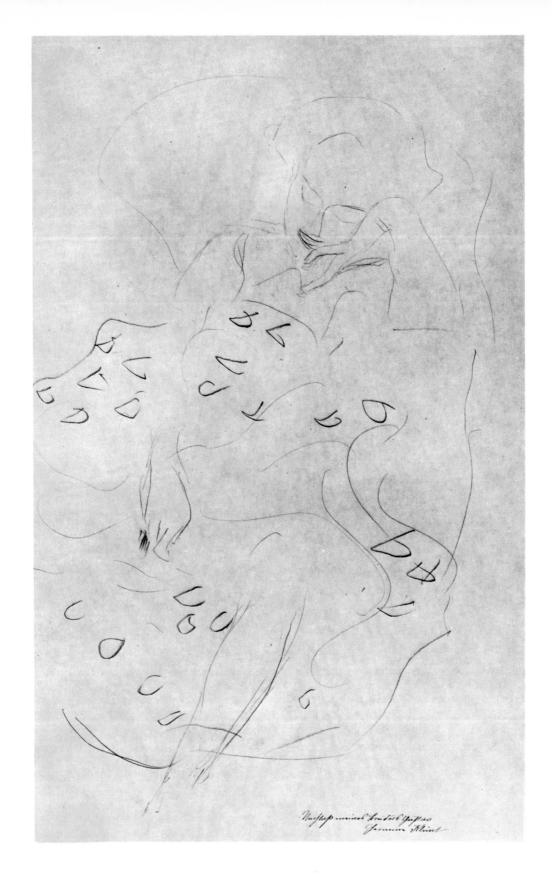

Plate 27. Gustav Klimt. *Girl Seated in a Chair*. 1906–7.

Plate 28. Egon Schiele. *Woman in Red Dress and Black Stockings.* 1911.

Plate 29. Gustav Klimt. *Mäda Primavesi*. Ca. 1912.   Plate 30. Gustav Klimt. *Portrait of Mäda Primavesi*. Ca. 1912.

Plate 31. Egon Schiele. *Black Girl.* 1911.

Plate 32. Egon Schiele. *Prostitute.* 1912.

Plate 33. Egon Schiele. *City on the Blue River (Study)*. 1910.

Plate 34. Egon Schiele. *Dead City I (Old City)*. 1912.

Plate 35. Gustav Klimt. *House in Garden (Forester's House in Weissenbach on the Attersee).* 1912.

Plate 36. Egon Schiele. *Stein on the Danube II (The Town of Stein)*. 1913.

Plate 37. Egon Schiele. *The Bridge (Study)*. 1913.

Plate 38. Egon Schiele. *The Bridge.* 1913.

Plate 39. Egon Schiele. *Self-Portrait with Brown Background.* 1912.

Plate 40. Egon Schiele. *Self-Portrait as St. Sebastian.* 1914.

Plate 41. Egon Schiele. *Nude Girl Sitting on Orange Cloth.* 1914.

Plate 42.
Egon Schiele.
*Woman in Green
Blouse with Muff.*
1915.

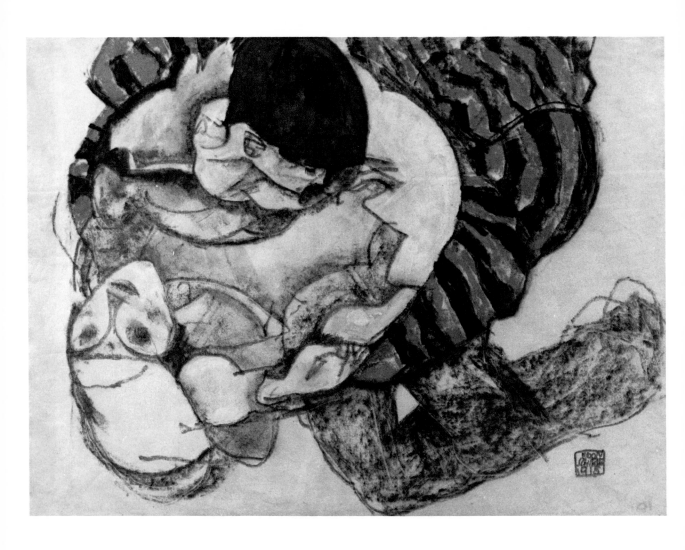

Plate 43. Egon Schiele. *The Embrace.* 1915.

Plate 44.
Egon Schiele.
*Portrait of the Artist's
Wife, Standing.* 1915.

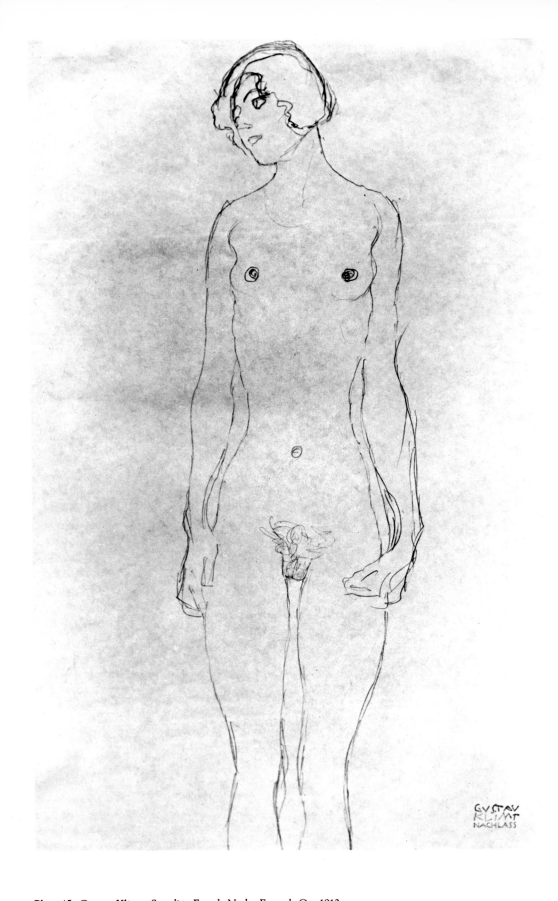

Plate 45. Gustav Klimt. *Standing Female Nude, Frontal.* Ca. 1912.

Plate 46. Gustav Klimt.
The Dancer. Ca. 1916–18.

Plate 47. Egon Schiele. *Russian Prisoner of War.* 1916.

Plate 48. Egon Schiele. *Portrait of an Old Man (Johann Harms)*. 1916.

Plate 50. Egon Schiele. *Portrait of the Artist's Nephew.* 1917.

Plate 49. Egon Schiele. *Portrait of the Artist's Wife, Seated.* 1917.

Plate 51. Egon Schiele. *Portrait of a Boy (The Artist's Nephew, Toni).* Ca. 1918.

Plate 52. Gustav Klimt. *Baby (Cradle)*. 1917–18.

Plate 53. Egon Schiele. *Reclining Nudes (Self-Portrait)*. Ca. 1918.

Plate 54. Egon Schiele. *Embrace (Lovers)*. Ca. 1917.

Plate 55. Egon Schiele. *Reclining Woman with Green Stockings.* 1917.   Plate 56. Egon Schiele. *Pottery.* 1918.

Plate 57. Egon Schiele. *Portrait of Victor Ritter von Bauer.* 1918.

Plate 58. Egon Schiele. *Portrait of the Painter Paris von Gütersloh*. 1918.

List of Plates

Kallir refers to Otto Kallir, *Egon Schiele—Oeuvre Catalogue of the Paintings*, Crown Publishers, New York/Paul Zsolnay Verlag, Vienna, 1966.

Novotny/Dobai refers to Fritz Novotny, Johannes Dobai, *Gustav Klimt* (with catalogue raisonné), Verlag Galerie Welz, Salzburg, 1967/Frederick A. Praeger, New York and Washington, 1968.

1. **Egon Schiele**
   Autumn Sun (Sunrise). 1912. Oil on canvas. Signed and dated (twice), center right. 31⅝″ × 31¾″ (80.2 × 80.5 cm). Kallir 165. Private collection.

2. **Gustav Klimt**
   Two Girls with Oleander. Ca. 1890–92. Oil on canvas. Signed, lower left. 21⅝″ × 50½″ (55 × 128.5 cm). Novotny/Dobai 59. Private collection.

3. **Gustav Klimt**
   Seated Lady. Ca. 1900. Red and blue crayon on paper. Estate stamp, lower right. 17″ × 11¾″ (43.2 × 29.8 cm). Collection Mr. and Mrs. Perry T. Rathbone.

4. **Gustav Klimt**
   Woman with Fur Collar. Ca. 1897–98. Oil on cardboard, mounted on wood. Signed, lower right. 14⅛″ × 7⅝″ (36 × 19.5 cm). Novotny/Dobai 80.

5. **Gustav Klimt**
   Portrait of a Woman in Profile. 1897–98. Pencil and red crayon on brownish paper. Estate stamp, lower right. 19″ × 14″ (48.2 × 35.5 cm). Collection Dr. and Mrs. Milton M. Gardner.

6. **Gustav Klimt**
   Seated Woman with Hat and Veil. 1897–98. Pencil on brown paper. Initialed, lower center. 17¾″ × 12¼″ (45 × 31 cm).

7. **Gustav Klimt**
   Moving Water. 1898. Oil on canvas. Signed, lower right. 21″ × 26⅛″ (53.3 × 66.3 cm). Novotny/Dobai 94. Private collection.

8. **Gustav Klimt**
   Island in the Attersee. Ca. 1901. Oil on canvas. Signed on the stretcher, upper left. 39⅜″ × 39⅜″ (100 × 100 cm). Novotny/Dobai 117. Estate of Dr. Otto Kallir.

9. **Gustav Klimt**
   The Park. Before 1910. Oil on canvas. Signed, lower left. 43¼″ × 43¼″ (110 × 110 cm). Novotny/Dobai 165. The Museum of Modern Art, New York; Gertrud A. Mellon Fund, 1957.

10. **Gustav Klimt**
    Pear Tree. 1903, later worked over. Mixed media, primarily oil, on canvas. 39″ × 39″ (99 × 99 cm). Novotny/Dobai 134. Busch-Reisinger Museum, Harvard University, Cambridge, Mass.; Gift of Dr. Otto Kallir, 1956.

11. **Gustav Klimt**
    Orchard (Garden Landscape). Before 1910. Oil and tempera on canvas. Signed, lower left. 39½″ × 39½″ (100.3 × 100.3 cm). Novotny/Dobai 164. Museum of Art, Carnegie Institute, Pittsburgh, 1960.

12. **Egon Schiele**
    Field of Flowers. 1910. Tempera and gold on paper. Initialed and dated, center right. 17½″ × 12⅛″ (44.2 × 30.7 cm). Kallir 122. Private collection.

13. **Gustav Klimt**
    Portrait of a Lady in Profile. 1904–5. Pencil, red and white crayon on Japan paper. Signed, lower right. Ca. 21⅛″ × 13⅜″ (ca. 53.5 × 34 cm). Collection Barbra Streisand.

14. **Gustav Klimt**
    Woman with Red Hair. 1908. Pencil, red and blue crayon on paper. Estate stamp, lower left. Ca. 21½″ × 14″ (ca. 54.5 × 35.5 cm). Collection Sir Rudolf Bing.

15. **Egon Schiele**
    Girl in a Plaid Garment. Ca. 1909. Black crayon and tempera on board. Initialed, lower left. 52¾″ × 20¾″ (134 × 52.7 cm). The Minneapolis Institute of Arts; Gift of Dr. Otto Kallir and The John R. van Derlip Fund, 1969.

16. **Egon Schiele**
    Standing Nude Girl. Ca. 1910. Watercolor and black chalk on paper. 17½″ × 12⅜″ (44.5 × 31.5 cm). Study for the painting *Female Nude Standing* (Kallir 110). Private collection.

17. **Gustav Klimt**

Three Courtesans. Ca. 1908. Pencil on paper. Signed, lower left. 22″ × 14½″ (56 × 37 cm). The Museum of Modern Art, New York; Mr. and Mrs. William B. Jaffe Fund, 1957.

18. **Gustav Klimt**

Hope II (Vision; Fertility; Legend). 1907–8. Oil on canvas. Signed, lower right. 43¼″ × 43¼″ (110 × 110 cm). Novotny/Dobai 155. The Museum of Modern Art, New York; Anonymous Donor and Mr. and Mrs. Ronald Lauder Fund, 1978.

19. **Gustav Klimt**

Lady with a Fan. 1903–4. Graphite on brown paper. Estate stamp, lower right. 18″ × 12¼″ (45.7 × 31 cm). Busch-Reisinger Museum, Harvard University, Cambridge, Mass.; Purchase in memory of Louis W. Black, 1959.

20. **Gustav Klimt**

Standing Lady in Profile. Ca. 1908. Pencil and red crayon on paper. Signed, lower left. 21⅛″ × 12½″ (53.5 × 31.7 cm). Collection Doctor and Mrs. Alvin D. Aisenberg.

21. **Gustav Klimt**

Seated Woman. Ca. 1914. Blue crayon on paper. Signed, lower center. 21¾″ × 14½″ (55.2 × 37 cm). Private collection.

22. **Egon Schiele**

Proletarian Girl in Black. 1910. Tempera and pencil on brownish paper. Initialed and dated, center right. 17¾″ × 12⅜″ (45 × 31.4 cm). Collection Mr. and Mrs. Jacob M. Kaplan.

23. **Egon Schiele**

Portrait of the Painter Zakovsek. 1910. Oil on canvas. Initialed and dated, lower left. 39⅜″ × 35⅜″ (100 × 89.8 cm). Kallir 102. Private collection.

24. **Egon Schiele**

Portrait of Dr. von Graff. 1910. Oil on canvas. Initialed and dated, lower left. 39⅜″ × 35½″ (100 × 90 cm). Kallir 101. Private collection.

25. **Egon Schiele**

Self-Portrait, Standing. 1910. Watercolor (black wash) and pencil on brownish paper. Signed and dated, lower left. 16¾″ × 10¾″ (42.5 × 27.3 cm).

26. **Egon Schiele**

Portrait of Eduard Kosmak. 1910. Tempera and black chalk on brown paper. Initialed and dated, lower right; inscribed "Kosmak," center right. 17⅝″ × 12″ (44.8 × 30.5 cm). Study for painting of the same title (Kallir 103). Collection Mr. and Mrs. Jacob M. Kaplan.

27. **Gustav Klimt**

Girl Seated in a Chair. 1906–7. Pencil on paper. Signed and inscribed, lower right, by the artist's sister, Hermine Klimt: "Nachlass meines Bruders Gustav" (Estate of my brother Gustav). 21⅝″ × 13¾″ (55 × 35 cm). The Solomon R. Guggenheim Museum, New York, 1967.

28. **Egon Schiele**

Woman in Red Dress and Black Stockings. 1911. Tempera and pencil on brownish paper. Initialed and dated, lower left. 18″ × 14″ (45.7 × 35.5 cm). The Fort Worth Art Museum; Gift of Mrs. Sue R. Pittman.

29. **Gustav Klimt**

Mäda Primavesi. Ca. 1912. Pencil on Japan paper. 22½″ × 14½″ (57 × 37 cm). Study for the painting *Portrait of Mäda Primavesi* (Novotny/Dobai 179). Private collection.

30. **Gustav Klimt**

Portrait of Mäda Primavesi. Ca. 1912. Oil on canvas. Signed, lower right. 59″ × 43¼″ (150 × 110 cm). Novotny/Dobai 179. Private collection.

31. **Egon Schiele**

Black Girl. 1911. Watercolor and graphite on brown paper. Signed and dated, lower left. 17¾″ × 14⅛″ (45 × 36 cm). Study for the painting of the same title (Kallir 125). Allen Memorial Art Museum, Oberlin College, Ohio; Friends of Art Fund, 1958.41.

32. **Egon Schiele**

Prostitute. 1912. Watercolor and pencil on Japan paper. Signed and dated, lower right. 19″ × 12⅜″

(48.2 × 31.4 cm). The Museum of Modern Art, New York; Mr. and Mrs. Donald B. Straus Fund, 1957.

33. **Egon Schiele**
City on the Blue River (Study). 1910. Tempera on paper. Signed and dated, lower right. 16¼″ × 12⅛″ (41.2 × 30.8 cm). Kallir 117. Private collection.

34. **Egon Schiele**
Dead City I (Old City). 1912. Oil on wood. Signed and dated, lower left. 16¾″ × 13⅜″ (42.5 × 34 cm). Kallir 167. Private collection.

35. **Gustav Klimt**
House in Garden (Forester's House in Weissenbach on the Attersee). 1912. Oil on canvas. Signed, lower left. 43¼″ × 43¼″ (110 × 110 cm). Novotny/Dobai 182. Private collection.

36. **Egon Schiele**
Stein on the Danube II (The Town of Stein). 1913. Oil on canvas. Signed and dated, lower right. 35⅜″ × 35¼″ (89.8 × 89.6 cm). Kallir 187. Private collection.

37. **Egon Schiele**
The Bridge (Study). 1913. Tempera, watercolor, and pencil on paper. Signed and dated, lower right. 12½″ × 19″ (31.7 × 48.2 cm). Study for painting of the same title (Kallir 181).

38. **Egon Schiele**
The Bridge. 1913. Oil on canvas. Signed and dated, lower left. 35¼″ × 35⅜″ (89.7 × 90 cm). Kallir 181. Estate of Dr. Otto Kallir.

39. **Egon Schiele**
Self-Portrait with Brown Background. 1912. Tempera, watercolor, and pencil on paper. Signed and dated, center left. 12⅜″ × 10″ (31.4 × 25.4 cm). Study for the painting Self-Portrait 1912 I (Kallir 151). Private collection.

40. **Egon Schiele**
Self-Portrait as St. Sebastian. 1914. Pencil on paper. Signed and dated, lower right. 12¾″ × 19″ (32.4 × 48.2 cm). Private collection.

41. **Egon Schiele**
Nude Girl Sitting on Orange Cloth. 1914. Tempera

and black crayon on paper. Signed and dated, lower right. Private collection.

42. **Egon Schiele**
Woman in Green Blouse with Muff. 1915. Tempera and black chalk on paper. Signed and dated, lower right. 18¾″ × 12″ (47.6 × 30.5 cm). Collection Mrs. Paul Sampliner.

43. **Egon Schiele**
The Embrace. 1915. Watercolor, charcoal, and crayon on paper. Signed and dated, lower right. 12¾″ × 17¾″ (32.4 × 45 cm). Collection Margaret Mallory.

44. **Egon Schiele**
Portrait of the Artist's Wife, Standing. 1915. Oil on canvas. Signed and dated, lower right. 70¾″ × 43¼″ (180 × 110 cm). Kallir 205. Haags Gemeentemuseum, The Hague, 1927–28.

45. **Gustav Klimt**
Standing Female Nude, Frontal. Ca. 1912. Pencil on Japan paper. Estate stamp, lower right. 22⅜″ × 14¾″ (56.8 × 37.5 cm). The Solomon R. Guggenheim Museum, New York, 1967.

46. **Gustav Klimt**
The Dancer. Ca. 1916–18. Oil on canvas. 70¾″ × 35½″ (180 × 90 cm). Novotny/Dobai 208. Private collection.

47. **Egon Schiele**
Russian Prisoner of War. 1916. Pencil and gouache on Japan paper. Signed and dated, lower right. Signed by the prisoner in Russian script, upper right. Verso: Standing Nude Couple, pencil. 19″ × 12⅛″ (48.2 × 30.7 cm). The Art Institute of Chicago; Given in memory of Gloria Brackstone Solow by Dr. Eugene Solow and Family.

48. **Egon Schiele**
Portrait of an Old Man (Johann Harms). 1916. Oil with wax on canvas. Signed and dated, lower right. 55⅛″ × 43½″ (140 × 110.4 cm). Kallir 213. The Solomon R. Guggenheim Museum, New York; Partial Gift, Dr. and Mrs. Otto Kallir, New York, 1969.

49. **Egon Schiele**
    Portrait of the Artist's Wife, Seated. 1917. Tempera and black chalk on paper. Signed and dated, lower center. 18¼″ × 11½″ (46.3 × 29.2 cm). Private collection.

50. **Egon Schiele**
    Portrait of the Artist's Nephew. 1917. Tempera, watercolor, and black chalk on paper. Signed and dated, lower left. 15″ × 10¼″ (38 × 26 cm). Study for the painting *Portrait of a Boy (The Artist's Nephew, Toni)* (Kallir 238). Private collection.

51. **Egon Schiele**
    Portrait of a Boy (The Artist's Nephew, Toni). Ca. 1918. Oil on canvas. With additions by another hand. 39⅛″ × 27½″ (99.4 × 70 cm). Kallir 238. Private collection.

52. **Gustav Klimt**
    Baby (Cradle). 1917–18. Oil and tempera on canvas. Unfinished. 43¼″ × 43¼″ (110 × 110 cm). Novotny/Dobai 221. National Gallery of Art, Washington, D.C.; Gift of Otto and Franziska Kallir and the Carol and Edwin Gaines Fullinwider Fund, 1978.

53. **Egon Schiele**
    Reclining Nudes (Self-Portrait). Ca. 1918. Charcoal on paper. 11¼″ × 17⅜″ (28.5 × 44 cm). The National Gallery of Canada, Ottawa, 1974.

54. **Egon Schiele**
    Embrace (Lovers). Ca. 1917. Oil on canvas. 39⅜″ × 67″ (100 × 170.2 cm). Kallir 224. Oesterreichische Galerie, Vienna.

55. **Egon Schiele**
    Reclining Woman with Green Stockings. 1917. Tempera and black chalk on paper. Signed and dated, lower right. 11″ × 17¾″ (28 × 45 cm), sight. Private collection.

56. **Egon Schiele**
    Pottery. 1918. Tempera, watercolor, and charcoal on paper. Signed, dated, and inscribed "O.W." (Ober Waltersdorf), lower left. 17″ × 11½″ (43.2 × 29.2 cm). Private collection.

57. **Egon Schiele**
    Portrait of Victor Ritter von Bauer. 1918. Oil on canvas. Signed and dated, lower right. 55⅜″ × 43¼″ (140.6 × 109.8 cm). Kallir 233. Oesterreichische Galerie, Vienna.

58. **Egon Schiele**
    Portrait of the Painter Paris von Gütersloh. 1918. Oil on canvas. Signed and dated, lower right. 55¼″ × 43¼″ (140.3 × 109.9 cm). Kallir 234. The Minneapolis Institute of Arts; Gift of P. D. McMillan Land Company, 1954.

Notes

1. "Saved from Europe," *New York Herald Tribune*, July 7, 1940.

2. "Reviews and Previews: Egon Schiele," *Art News*, March, 1965.

3. Johannes Dobai: "Gustav Klimt—Art Nouveau Painter," p. 20, and Thomas M. Messer: "Gustav Klimt and Egon Schiele," p. 10, in the exhibition catalogue *Gustav Klimt and Egon Schiele*, The Solomon R. Guggenheim Museum, New York, 1965.

4. Charlotte Lichtblau: "12 Years of Egon Schiele—Intensity against Nothingness," *Philadelphia Inquirer*, November 3, 1968.

5. Herschel B. Chipp: "A Neglected Expressionist Movement—Vienna 1910–1924," *Artforum* I/9 (1963), p. 22.

6. Otto Kallir: *Egon Schiele—Oeuvre Catalogue of the Paintings*, Crown Publishers, New York/Paul Zsolnay Verlag, Vienna, 1966, and *The Graphic Work of Egon Schiele*, Crown Publishers, New York/Paul Zsolnay Verlag, Vienna, 1970.

7. Emily Genauer: "Exhibits from Italy and Austria," *New York Herald Tribune*, April 5, 1959.

8. "Reviews and Previews: Gustav Klimt," *Art News*, April, 1959.

9. "New Acquisitions," *Time Magazine*, June 13, 1955.

10. Thomas M. Messer: Preface to the exhibition catalogue *Egon Schiele 1890–1918*, Institute of Contemporary Art, Boston, 1960.

11. *Ibid.*

12. *New York Herald Tribune*, 1940, *op. cit.*

13. Sam Hunter: "A Pioneer Modernist," *New York Times*, April 11, 1948.

14. Peter Selz: "Egon Schiele," *Art International*, ca. December, 1960, p. 39.

15. Hilton Kramer: "An Elegant Charade," *New Leader*, March 1, 1965, p. 29.

16. "The Art of Egon Schiele," *Scene*, August 4, 1961, p. 40.

17. Alessandra Comini: *Gustav Klimt*, George Braziller, New York, 1975, and *Egon Schiele*, George Braziller, New York, 1976.

18. Hunter, *op. cit.*

19. John Simon: "Four Austrian Expressionists," *New York Times*, March 19, 1961.

20. One of the most devastating of these losses occurred when a group of major Klimt paintings (including the three University panels), which had been stored at Schloss Immendorf, was destroyed by retreating German soldiers.

21. Klimt's studies for the *Stoclet Frieze* (Novotny/Dobai 152) were lent to the Guggenheim for the 1965 show. In 1978, the Museum of Modern Art acquired *Hope II* (Pl. 18).

22. Otto Kallir (Nirenstein): *Egon Schiele—Persönlichkeit und Werk*, Paul Zsolnay Verlag, Berlin, Vienna, Leipzig, 1930.

23. *Das graphische Werk von Egon Schiele*, Introduction by Arthur Roessler, Rikola Verlag-Verlag Neuer Graphik, Vienna, Berlin, Leipzig, Munich, 1922.

24. Werner Hofmann: *Gustav Klimt*, New York Graphic Society, Boston, 1971.

25. Fritz Karpfen, ed.: *Das Egon Schiele Buch*, Wiener Graphische Werkstätte, Vienna, 1921, p. 85.

26. Felix Salten: "Gustav Klimt," in *Geister der Zeit—Erlebnisse*, Paul Zsolnay Verlag, Vienna, 1924, pp. 42–43.

27. Arthur Roessler, ed.: *Briefe und Prosa von Egon Schiele*, Richard Lanyi, Vienna, 1921, p. 97.

28. Dobai, *op. cit.*, p. 25.

29. See Klimt's *Judith I* (Novotny/Dobai 113) and *Water Serpents* (Novotny/Dobai 139).

30. Karpfen, *op. cit.*

List of Exhibitions

A selection of shows, featuring Klimt and Schiele, which Dr. Otto Kallir organized or to which he substantially contributed; authors of catalogue texts are listed in parentheses.

1921 **Internationale Schwarz-Weiss-Ausstellung.** Künstlerhaus, Salzburg. Original etching by Schiele in the deluxe edition of the catalogue.

1923 **Egon Schiele:** Paintings, watercolors, drawings. Neue Galerie, Vienna (Kurt Rathe).

1926 **Gustav Klimt.** Neue Galerie, Vienna.

1927–1928 **Oostenrijksche Schilderijen en Kunstnijverheid.** The Hague, Amsterdam, Rotterdam (Hans Tietze).

1928 **Gustav Klimt:** Paintings. Neue Galerie, Vienna.

1928 **Egon Schiele:** Paintings, watercolors, drawings. Hagenbund—Neue Galerie, Vienna (Bruno Grimschitz).

1930 **Unbekanntes von Egon Schiele.** Neue Galerie, Vienna.

1937 **Exposition d'Art Autrichien.** Jeu de Paume, Paris (Jean Mistler, Alfred Stix).

1941 **Egon Schiele:** Paintings, watercolors, drawings. Galerie St. Etienne, New York.

1945 **Austrian Paintings 1818–1918.** The American British Art Center, New York (Hans Tietze).

1945 **Klimt, Schiele, Kokoschka.** Neue Galerie, Vienna (Benno Fleischmann).

1948 **Egon Schiele:** Paintings, watercolors, drawings. Galerie St. Etienne, New York (Joseph von Sternberg).

1948 **Egon Schiele:** Paintings. Neue Galerie, Vienna (Otto Kallir–Nirenstein).

1957 **Egon Schiele:** Watercolors, drawings. Galerie St. Etienne, New York (Otto Benesch).

1959 **Gustav Klimt:** Paintings. Galerie St. Etienne, New York (Otto Kallir).

1960–1961 **Egon Schiele:** Paintings, watercolors, drawings. Institute of Contemporary Art, Boston; Galerie St. Etienne, New York; Speed Museum, Louisville; Carnegie Institute, Pittsburgh; Minneapolis Institute of Arts (Thomas M. Messer, Otto Kallir).

1963 **Viennese Expressionism 1910–1924.** University of California, Berkeley; Pasadena Art Museum (Herschel B. Chipp).

1963–1964 **Austrian Expressionists.** Galerie St. Etienne, New York; Sarasota Art Association; Fort Worth Art Center.

1965 **Gustav Klimt and Egon Schiele:** Paintings, watercolors, drawings. The Solomon R. Guggenheim Museum, New York (Thomas M. Messer, Johannes Dobai, James Demetrion, Alessandra Comini).

1965 **Egon Schiele:** Watercolors, drawings. Galerie St. Etienne, New York (Thomas M. Messer).

1967 **Fifty Drawings by Gustav Klimt.** Galerie St. Etienne, New York.

1968 **Egon Schiele:** Watercolors, drawings. Galerie St. Etienne, New York (Otto Benesch, Otto Kallir).

1969 **Creative Austria—20th Century.** Philadelphia Civic Center.

1970 **Gustav Klimt:** Drawings. Galerie St. Etienne, New York (Gustav Glück, Fritz Novotny).

1975 **Egon Schiele:** Paintings, watercolors, drawings. Haus der Kunst, Munich (Thomas M. Messer).